SNOWBOARDING

CHERRY
LAKE
Publishing

Published in the United States of America by Cherry Lake Publishing
Ann Arbor, Michigan
www.cherrylakepublishing.com

Content Adviser: Liv Williams, Editor, www.iLivExtreme.com
Reading Adviser: Marla Conn MS, Ed., Literacy specialist, Read-Ability, Inc.

Photo Credits: ©mjaud / Shutterstock.com, cover; ©tuyoshi / Shutterstock.com, 5; ©mark6mauno / flickr.com, 7; ©Iurii Osadchi / Shutterstock.com, 9; ©Alfaguarilla / Shutterstock.com, 10; ©mountainpix / Shutterstock.com, 13, 15; ©NatalieJean / Shutterstock.com, 14; ©Mitch Gunn / Shutterstock.com, 16; ©Kvanta / Shutterstock.com, 19; ©ERainbow / Shutterstock.com, 20; ©Sergei Bachlakov / Shutterstock.com, 21; ©Daniel Koell / Shutterstock.com, 22; ©Vlad Zaytsev / Shutterstock.com, 25; ©BestStockFoto / Shutterstock.com, 26; ©Photographed by Thatcher Cook for PopTech / PopTech / flickr.com, 27; ©Photo: GEPA pictures/ Christopher Kelemen / Special Olympics 2017 / flickr.com / Public Domain, 28

Library of Congress Cataloging-in-Publication Data

Names: Labrecque, Ellen, author.
Title: Snowboarding / by Ellen Labrecque.
Description: Ann Arbor, Michigan : Cherry Lake Publishing, 2018. | Series: Global citizens: Olympic sports |
    Includes bibliographical references and index.
Identifiers: LCCN 2017031117 | ISBN 9781534107496 (hardcover) | ISBN 9781534109476 (pdf) |
    ISBN 9781534108486 (pbk.) | ISBN 9781534120464 (hosted ebook)
Subjects: LCSH: Snowboarding—Juvenile literature. | Winter Olympics—Juvenile literature.
Classification: LCC GV857.S57 L33 2018 | DDC 796.939—dc23
LC record available at https://lccn.loc.gov/2017031117

Cherry Lake Publishing would like to acknowledge the work of The Partnership for 21st Century Learning.
Please visit *www.p21.org* for more information.

Printed in the United States of America
Corporate Graphics

ABOUT THE AUTHOR

Ellen Labrecque has written over 100 books for children. She loves the Olympics and has attended both the Winter and Summer Games as a reporter for magazines and television. She lives in Yardley, Pennsylvania, with her husband, Jeff, and her two young "editors," Sam and Juliet. When she isn't writing, she is running, hiking, and reading.

TABLE OF CONTENTS

CHAPTER 1

History: Snowboarding

The first Winter Olympics was held in Chamonix, France, from January 25 to February 5, 1924. It included 258 athletes from 16 different countries competing in 16 events. Since then, the Winter Olympics has been held every 4 years in a number of countries. (The Games were skipped in 1940 and 1944 during World War II.) As the Games progressed, more competitors and events were added. Fast-forward to the 2014 Winter Games held in Sochi, Russia. There were 2,873 competitors from 88 different countries competing in 98 events. That's a lot more competitors and events!

From jaw-dropping aerial flips in skiing to lightning-speed action in hockey, the Winter Games display some of the most unbelievable sports and athletes. Snowboarding, since its invention

There were 69 men and 56 women Olympic snowboarders
competing at the 1998 Games in Nagano, Japan.

and introduction to the Olympics, showcases one of the most
heart-stopping and thrilling competitions in the Winter Olympics.

The Story of Snowboarding

Snowboarding didn't become a sport in the Winter Olympics
until the 1998 Games in Nagano, Japan. In fact, the first official
snowboard **prototype** didn't appear until 33 years earlier.
Sherman Poppen of Muskegon, Michigan, attached two skis
together to make one giant board. His wife named the board the
"Snurfer." Unlike the snowboards we see today, the Snurfer did

not have **bindings** that secured the rider to the board. Instead, the riders held on to a rope in front to keep their balance.

In 1972, Dimitrije Milovich and Wayne Stoveken had a similar idea. But instead of skis, they were influenced by surfboards. They started their own company called Winterstick and began selling their "Snow Surfboards" out of a shop in Salt Lake City, Utah. Unlike the Snurfer, these boards included foot straps to help the rider stay on the board.

A decade later, the first snowboarding competition took place in Vermont. Snowboarders cruised down mountains as fast as 50 miles (80.5 kilometers) per hour. The event continued to be held every year at resorts in Vermont, and in 1985, it was renamed the US Open Snowboarding Championships.

At first, ski resort owners didn't want snowboarders on their slopes. They wanted only skiers to use the mountains. But they soon changed their minds when they realized how popular snowboarding was becoming. In 1985, only 40 US resorts allowed snowboarders. By 1990, 476 resorts allowed them! In 2017, only three ski resorts in North America—two in Utah and one in Vermont—banned snowboarders from flying down their mountains.

The Brighton Resort in Utah displays the evolution of snowboards over the years.

The Pipe Dragon

Snowboarders didn't just want to race down mountains. They also wanted to do tricks in the air. Many snowboarders used snow shovels to build ramps and **half-pipes**. But Doug Waugh, a farmer from Colorado, came up with an easier way. In 1990, Waugh invented the Pipe Dragon out of old farming equipment. The Pipe Dragon was a grooming machine with rotating blades that could cut walls 10 to 12 feet (3 to 3.6 meters) high out of the snow. Over the next 8 years, Waugh and his Pipe Dragon built more than 120 pipes for resorts around the world. He was also the official pipe builder for the 1998 Winter Olympics in Nagano, Japan, when snowboarding made its debut.

[21ST CENTURY SKILLS LIBRARY]

Kaitlyn Farrington of Utah brought home gold
for the half-pipe event at the 2014 Sochi Games.

In snowboard cross, which is also known as boardercross,
four to six athletes race down a steep and narrow course.

Snowboarding Events

At the 1998 Games, there were only two snowboarding events for men and women: the **giant slalom** and the half-pipe. Since then, a few more snowboarding events for men and women have been added: **snowboard cross**, **parallel slalom**, **giant parallel slalom** (replacing giant slalom), **slopestyle**, and team ski-snowboard cross. A new event called **big air** will be introduced at the 2018 Winter Games in PyeongChang, South Korea.

Developing Claims and Using Evidence

Big air is a competition where snowboarders ride down a giant ramp and fly into the air to do tricks. The ramp at the 2018 Olympics is 160 feet (49 m) high—the tallest in the world! Athletes are judged on how big, how daring, and how perfect each trick is. The riskier the trick, the higher the rider's score will be. Some fans say snowboarders shouldn't risk their lives to win gold. Other fans say the riskier and more exciting, the better snowboarding is to watch. Has snowboarding at the Olympics become too dangerous? Why or why not? Use the Internet and your local library to gather information. Form an opinion based on your findings.

CHAPTER 2

Geography: Not Everybody Snowboards

At the 2014 Winter Olympics, 243 athletes from 31 nations participated in at least one of the snowboarding events. Not surprisingly, not one country in Africa had an athlete competing. After all, Africa is the world's hottest continent and home to the Sahara, one of the world's largest deserts. Brazil, a country known more for its sandy beaches than for its snow, had only one athlete, Isabel Clark Ribeiro, compete in an event.

So where do the best snowboarders in the world come from? Which countries have won the most Olympic snowboarding medals?

Ribeiro competed in the 2006, 2010, and 2014 Winter Olympics.

White is not only a professional snowboarder,
but also a professional skateboarder!

United States

The United States has won more medals, including more gold medals, than any other country in snowboarding at the Winter Olympics. As of 2017, the US team has won 24 medals total. The United States is also the only country with two athletes who have won double gold medals in snowboarding—Shaun White and Seth Wescott. White won both of his gold medals in the half-pipe at the 2006 and 2010 Games. Wescott won both of his gold medals in snowboard cross, also at the 2006 and 2010 Games.

[21ST CENTURY SKILLS LIBRARY]

Wescott learned how to ski first before switching to snowboarding.

Christian Haller (pictured) and his sister Ursina Haller competed for Switzerland at the 2014 Games.

Switzerland

Switzerland is right behind the United States when it comes to winning Olympic snowboarding medals. The country has taken home 12 medals total, including seven gold. The Swiss star on the slopes is Philipp Schoch, who won gold medals in giant parallel slalom at the 2002 and 2006 Winter Olympics. At the 2006 Games, Schoch beat his brother, Simon, for gold by just .88 seconds!

Gathering and Evaluating Sources

As of the 2018 Games, there will have been 23 Winter Olympics held since it was established in 1924. In the 23 Games held, only two have been hosted in a country south of the equator. This was during the 1956 and 2000 Games in Australia. Using the Internet and your local library, research reasons why the Olympic committee overlooks countries in the lower half of the hemisphere. Use the data you find to support your claim.

CHAPTER 3

Civics: Olympic Pride

Hosting the Olympic Games can be a big source of pride for the city and the people who live there. It gives the citizens a chance to show off where they live to the entire world. Through news articles and television, viewers learn all about the host country and city. One of the biggest ways the host country shows off is at the opening and closing ceremonies.

Snowboarder Johnny Lyall was the biggest star of the 2010 Winter Olympics in Vancouver, Canada. At the opening ceremonies, Lyall, a Vancouver native, snowboarded down a ramp and flew through one of the giant Olympic rings. He rode smoothly down a ramp on the other side. Then with a big smile, he welcomed everybody to the Games.

Athletes and coaches march side by side during the Parade of Nations, a traditional part of the opening ceremony.

Snowboarding Popularity

More than 5 million people in the United States and over 1 million people in Canada snowboard every year. The US figure has actually declined by 1 million since 2007, which has been blamed in part by a lack of snow and warmer winters due to **climate change**. But even if fewer people were actually snowboarding, they still love to watch it at the Olympics.

The United States, Norway, and Canada are the top snowboarding destinations.

The 2010 snowboarding events were held at Cypress Mountain in Vancouver, Canada.

At the 2010 Games, Shaun White's performance on the slopes drew the largest number of viewers—30.1 million—for NBC, the station broadcasting the Games! In 2014, his performance was live-streamed by 600,000 viewers, the highest Winter Olympics live-stream that year. Snowboarding was also one of the top searched terms on the Internet during the 2010 Games.

Beijing, China, the host city for the 2022 Games, will rely almost entirely on artificial snow.

Gold Isn't the New Green

While the popularity of the Winter Games keeps growing, it is getting harder to find host cities that get enough snow for events like snowboarding. Olympic cities can make their own snow, but it has to be cold enough to keep the snow from melting after it's made.

The 2010 Vancouver and 2014 Sochi Winter Olympics were the warmest in history, and both cities struggled to keep snow on the ground. During the Vancouver Games, the city had to helicopter in snow almost every 5 minutes! In Sochi, snowboarders had to shift practice times due to the unusually warm weather. Scientists predict that by 2080 only six out of the 19 previous winter host cities will be cold enough to host the Winter Games if this warming trend continues.

Developing Claims

Protect Our Winters is a winter sports community working against climate change. Professional snowboarder Jeremy Jones started this organization. Go to protectourwinters.org to read all about their goals and mission. Using evidence you find, form your own ideas about what you can do to stop climate change.

CHAPTER 4

Economics: Snowboarding Is Big Business

Hosting the Olympic Games costs a lot of money. Reports revealed that the 2014 Winter Olympics cost the host city of Sochi over $50 billion! The city earned back some of this money once the Games began through a number of ways.

The Fans

Tourists come to the city to see the Olympics. They spend money on hotels, souvenirs, and restaurants. Snowboarding is the Winter Olympics' biggest draw—and why wouldn't it be? It is a combination of cool athletes and a thrilling sport. You can't beat it from a spectator's point of view. The more people who come and watch snowboarding, the more money the city gets.

Russia had a budget of $12 billion for the 2014 Games.
They overspent by $38 billion!

Burton Snowboards and Canada Snowboard are partnering to help outfit the Olympic Canadian snowboarding team.

The Sponsors

Advertisers like Coca-Cola, McDonald's, and BP, an energy company, pay a lot of money to sponsor the Olympics and **Paralympics**. Their signs and logos appear on television in commercials and on boards all over the **venues**. Clothing companies supply the uniforms and the outfits for the opening and closing ceremonies. Burton Snowboards made the uniforms for the US snowboarders at the last three Games. "The uniforms are designed around feedback from some of the best American snowboarders to make sure that the design, fit, and vibe

Coca-Cola is sponsoring four athletes during the 2018 Games including Amy Purdy, a US Paralympic snowboarder.

Hannah Teter is one of the highest paid Olympic snowboarders in the United States.

Taking Informed Action

Do you want to learn more about the Winter Olympics and snowboarding? There are many different organizations that you can explore. Check them out online. Here are three to start your search:

- *USSA—Snowboarding: Learn more about the US Snowboarding Team on its official website.*
- *Team USA—Snowboarding: Read about the athletes and qualifications for the US Olympic Team.*
- *Olympic—Snowboarding: Find out more about the previous and upcoming snowboarding Olympic events.*

represented our sport and our country in the best possible way," explained Jake Burton, the head of Burton Snowboards.

Snowboarders Can Make Big Bucks

Snowboarders around the world can make a lot of money—much more than a lot of the other Winter Olympians. Why? Their sport is the most popular one. Companies are willing to pay snowboarders more money to advertise their products. And when snowboarders compete in the Olympics and win medals, they'll likely earn even more money from sponsors. Shaun White is one of the highest paid snowboarders in history. He has made more than $20 million in his career!

Communicating Conclusions

Before reading this book, did you know much about snowboarding and the Winter Olympics? Now that you know more, do you think snowboarders should always try to go bigger and faster? Do you think the bigger and faster they go, the more dangerous the sport could be? Share what you learned with friends at school or with your family.

Think About It

Snowboarding was invented in the United States and made its debut at the 1998 Games. There were a total of four events: men's and women's half-pipe and giant slalom. However, despite inventing the sport, the United States only placed third in the men's and the women's half-pipe. Why do you think Canada, Switzerland, France, and Germany placed first in the four snowboarding events instead of the United States? Use the Internet and your local library to find more information. Use the data you find to support your answer.

For More Information

Further Reading

Bailer, Darice. *Snowboard Cross*. Minneapolis: Lerner Publications, 2014.

Wallechinsky, David, and Jaime Loucky. *The Complete Book of the Winter Olympics*. Hertford, NC: Crossroad Press, 2014.

Waxman, Laura Hamilton. *Snowboarding*. Mankato, MN: Amicus Ink, 2017.

Websites

The International Olympic Committee
https://www.olympic.org/the-ioc
Discover how the IOC works to build a better world through sports.

TransWorld SNOWboarding
http://snowboarding.transworld.net
Learn more about the snowboarding culture.

GLOSSARY

big air (BIG AIR) athletes jump off ramps as high as 160 feet (49 meters) and perform a trick in the air

bindings (BINDE-ingz) devices that hold a boot firmly to a ski or snowboard

climate change (KLYE-mit CHAYNJ) a change in normal weather patterns over a long period of time

giant parallel slalom (JYE-uhnt PAR-uh-lel SLAH-lohm) a speed race where snowboarders weave through a course of gates and tight turns (longer run and with more gates than parallel slalom); this event replaced the original giant slalom event

giant slalom (JYE-uhnt SLAH-lohm) competitors race downhill against each other

half-pipes (HAF-pipes) long half cylinders made of snow and ice for doing tricks in snowboarding; also an event in snowboarding where athletes do tricks in the air

parallel slalom (PAR-uh-lel SLAH-lohm) a speed race where snowboarders weave through a course of gates and tight turns (shorter run and with less gates than giant parallel slalom)

Paralympics (par-uh-LIM-piks) an international competition, like the Olympics, but for physically disabled athletes

prototype (PROH-tuh-tipe) the first version of an invention that tests an idea to see if it will work

slopestyle (SLOHP-stile) a race where riders go down an obstacle course and try to do the hardest tricks for the highest scores

snowboard cross (SNOH-bord KRAWS) an event where four snowboarders start at the same time and race through a course filled with obstacles, ramps, turns, and jumps

tourists (TOOR-ists) people who are traveling for pleasure

venues (VEN-yooz) places where actions or events occur

INDEX